DEVELOPMENT WITHOUT DAMAGE

Building Homes for Tomorrow

Rob Bowden

A⁺
Smart Apple Media

Building homes for tomorrow /
728 BOW

12800

Bowden. Rob.

1. Most items may be checked out for two weeks and renewed for the same period. Additional restrictions may apply to high demand items.

2. A fine is charged for each school day material is not returned according to the above rule.

3. All damage to materials beyond reasonable wear and all losses shall be paid for by the borrower.

4. Each borrower is responsible for all items checked out on his/her library record and for all fines accruing on the same.

5. Library privileges may be restricted for borrowers who do not return overdue material or pay their fines in a timely fashion.

DEMCO

Contents

Introduction

In 2008, there were estimated to be nearly 6.7 billion people on Earth, but where and how they live varies greatly. Some people live in large houses with every modern convenience at their disposal. Greater numbers of people live in smaller homes or apartment buildings, but they still enjoy a good quality of life. For millions, however, home is little more than a basic shelter. Some people have no home at all. One of the greatest challenges we face in the twenty-first century is providing housing for a growing global population without placing further pressure on the environment and already limited resources.

Living Conditions

Many of us take for granted the fact that we have a home—a roof over our heads, a place to eat and sleep, and shelter. We have lighting, heating, and running water. This is not the case all over the world, though. It is estimated that more than 1.6 billion people in less economically developed countries (LEDCs) have inadequate housing. Often conditions are overcrowded, and water quality and sanitation is poor. Even in more economically developed countries (MEDCs), there are people who live in poverty, in poor-quality housing.

Problems and Shortages

The difficulty is that governments cannot simply build more houses and provide communities with clean water supplies. To begin with, the countries with the most people in poor housing are often the ones that do not have the money to build more sustainable communities. Even if the money was available to provide settlements like those in Europe or North America, building them would place a huge strain on resources. There is simply not enough land, building materials, energy, or water for all people to live in this way.

At the beginning of the twentieth century, the population of the world was 1.6 billion. Today it is nearly 6.7 billion.

Slum conditions in Nairobi, Kenya. Across the world, more than a billion people live in such conditions.

Facing the Challenge

The world's population is expected to reach nine billion by 2050, so solving the global housing crisis is a pressing issue. To face the challenge, governments and organizations all over the world are looking at many different factors. These include the materials used to build houses, ways of saving energy in homes, and making sustainable homes affordable for more people.

But building individual homes is just one part of a bigger drive toward sustainable housing development. To truly solve the problem, people are looking at how whole communities—from villages to cities—are planned and built. For everyone to have a secure and healthy home, experts are now thinking about how those homes will fit into sustainable communities. They are considering issues such as land use, how public buildings can be used, and infrastructures like waste disposal and transport systems. All around the world, there are examples of how homes and communities can be built more sustainably. These models provide ideas and experiences from which others can learn. They show that it is possible to achieve development without damage.

EXPERT VIEW

"Everyone has the right to a standard of living adequate for the health and well-being of himself and of his family, including food, clothing, housing, and medical care and necessary social services, and the right to security in the event of unemployment, sickness, disability, widowhood, old age, or other lack of livelihood in circumstances beyond his control."
ARTICLE 25(I), UNIVERSAL DECLARATION OF HUMAN RIGHTS

The Global Housing Crisis

The world is facing a housing crisis. In less developed regions such as Africa, Asia, and Latin America, there are thought to be around one billion people living in poor-quality housing in towns and cities. Millions more live in rural homes that do not have basic services such as clean water and sanitation. In more developed regions such as Europe and North America, fewer people live in such conditions, but millions of people struggle with the cost of housing. What has caused the global housing crisis and what can be done to address the problem?

Population Growth

In the middle of the twentieth century, the population of the world was 2.5 billion. Over the next 50 years, the population grew faster than at any time in history—to more than six billion people by 2000. Experts believe that by 2050, there will be nine billion people in the world. Keeping pace with the housing needs of such a fast-growing population is extremely difficult.

The Problems of Urbanization

In the past, more people lived in rural areas than in towns and cities. In 2007, the world's urban population exceeded its rural one for the first time. By 2050, it is thought that 75 percent of us will live in urban areas. The process by which populations become concentrated in towns and cities is called "urbanization."

One of the biggest problems of urbanization is the speed at which it is happening. In 2008, for example, the population of Mumbai, India, increased at a rate of 47 people every hour. How can authorities find suitable housing quickly for so many people, particularly when they are among the very poorest in the country? What happens in many of these cases is that people end up

Mumbai has a population of 19 million people, and more than half of them live in makeshift houses in slums and shantytowns.

homeless on the city streets, or they settle on the outskirts of the cities in slums or shantytowns. These are not planned residential areas, so often they do not have services such as waste disposal or clean water supplies, which means that disease can spread easily. Houses are temporary structures built from whatever people can find. Local authorities do not like shantytowns because pollution and crime rates are high, but the people who live there often have nowhere else to go.

Even in MEDCs, urbanization is a problem. There might be better-quality housing available, and the people moving to the cities might have more money to pay for it, but more people means higher levels of pollution, more crime, and higher unemployment—the same problems that are faced by authorities in less developed countries.

Urban Sprawl

Another problem related to urbanization is known as "urban sprawl." This is the process by which cities gradually expand into outlying areas, growing larger and larger as populations increase. Land that was once green and relatively unpopulated is lost to building development as cities grow. There are a number of cities around the world that have grown so much that they are now known as "megacities"—places that have populations of more than 10 million. Tokyo (Japan), New York (United States), and Mexico City (Mexico) are all megacities.

FACTS IN FOCUS
Ever-Growing Numbers

Between 2000 and 2008, the world's population increased at an average of 149 people every minute. To provide them all with housing would require building a city of a million people every five days! In reality, population growth is spread out across the world and takes place at different rates. The world's least developed countries in Africa and Asia are experiencing the most rapid growth. Population growth in more developed regions is much slower and makes up only around five percent of expected future growth.

As more and more people move to already large urban areas like Mexico City, previously undeveloped land gets taken over by planned housing or by unplanned shantytowns.

The Potential of Urbanization

The impacts of urbanization may not appear to offer much hope for a sustainable future, but there is another, more positive side to the process. By concentrating people in a single location, urbanization has the potential to solve problems of poverty and environmental damage. It provides opportunities to build lower-cost shared housing and to offer more efficient services such as public transportation and waste management, which are less damaging to the environment.

Across the world, there are examples of cities responding to the opportunities of urbanization.

In South Africa, several cities are developing low-cost urban housing to improve the lives of the country's millions of slum dwellers. In the poor township of Lwandle, near Cape Town, for example, the People's Housing Project allows residents to offset the cost of buying a new home by getting them involved in construction. They can provide their own labor and use materials that they already own, which makes the overall cost much less. The program has also fitted more than 600 existing houses with solar water heaters to help reduce energy costs for the residents.

CASE STUDY

Brazil: Curitiba

Curitiba in Brazil is one of the best examples of a city responding to the potential of urbanization. In the 1970s, the new mayor put forward a plan to renovate the city through policies of sustainable development, based around a series of public transportation corridors that provide fast and low-cost bus travel around the city. The authorities set aside a large piece of land and began a program in which people could buy a plot to build on. The people built their homes themselves, but free advice was offered from architects on how to plan and construct the houses. Increasing numbers of people moved out of the shantytowns and into better, more integrated housing. People do still live in slum areas around the city, but there are far fewer than there were just a few years ago. In 2008, Curitiba was recognized as one of the most sustainable cities in the world by the Ethisphere Institute, an organization that works toward ethical and socially responsible development.

The transportation system in Curitiba has improved the quality of life of the city's inhabitants by reducing the amount of pollution caused by private car ownership.

In Lwandle, a shantytown near Cape Town in South Africa, plans are under way to replace temporary housing with safe, sustainable homes.

The Big Picture

Sustainable housing projects are providing homes for people all over the world, but there are problems associated with all this new building. Each new home requires building materials, energy, water, and waste facilities. If these projects are to be successful, planning must extend to the wider community. Buses and trains are needed to link homes to places of work, leisure, and shopping, for example. All this places great pressure on resources.

When considering sustainable development in urban or rural areas, it is important to see the big picture and to think about the environmental impact of the building industry. This involves everything from the choice of the materials used to build homes and how much energy is used in the construction process, to the amount of energy it takes to keep the home running. There are also considerations that affect whole communities, such as the need for access to green spaces like parks and gardens to provide a better quality of life, and finding ways to limit traffic pollution.

So, how can individual homes and, indeed, whole communities be developed in a sustainable way? The key is careful planning.

EXPERT VIEW

"There are those who . . . depict cities as hopeless places where a person cannot breathe, move, or live properly due to excess population and automobiles. I, however, do not share these views. My professional experience has taught me that cities are not problems, they are solutions. So I can face an urban world only with optimism."

JAIME LERNER, FORMER MAYOR OF CURITIBA, 2007

Sustainable Homes

Whether a megacity of 15 million people or a village of 100, the individual home is at the heart of any community. It is therefore important to get the type of house right for the people who will live there. This is not as simple as it sounds, though. Location, design, materials, cost, ownership, and how a home is used are all factors to consider when planning a sustainable house.

Early Shelters

For many thousands of years, houses were built using natural materials such as stone, earth, wood, reeds, and plants. People could build shelters from these materials quickly, and it did not require much skill. They did not last as long as many modern homes, but that did not matter. It was simple to knock them down and build a new one. At the end of their life, all the materials could be returned back to the Earth, making these early homes completely recyclable. In many LEDCs, simple construction methods like these are still used, especially in rural areas.

The seminomadic Maasai people of Kenya still live in temporary shelters made of mud and branches.

Transporting new building materials like concrete to construction sites contributes to pollution.

The Revolution in Building Materials

In the eighteenth century, machines were invented that allowed goods to be made more efficiently and in greater numbers. This Industrial Revolution also led to the development of new, man-made building materials such as iron and brick. By the late nineteenth century, these materials were being used much more than the traditional, natural materials for building houses. In the twentieth century, even better materials were invented that could be used for housing, including concrete and plastic.

The Environmental Cost

These developments changed the way homes were built. They allowed larger, longer-lasting houses to be constructed for less money. However, many of the more recent building materials are far from environmentally friendly. To begin with, they use enormous amounts of natural resources, and mining for these damages the environment. Concrete, for example, relies on minerals as its raw material. Although many of the minerals are common, they still need to be extracted from the ground, which can leave unsightly scars on the landscape. The processing of these materials uses a lot of energy and can cause pollution. Concrete production is responsible for around 10 percent of the world's carbon dioxide (CO_2) emissions—the main gas contributing to global warming.

Energy and pollution are also involved in transporting materials, whether in raw or processed form, to where they are needed. This can often be a long way from the original site. The building phase also requires energy. At the end of their life, many of these new materials can be difficult or expensive to recycle or dispose of.

Natural Walls

As part of plans to build more sustainable homes, many people are now choosing to revert to more traditional, natural materials like earth and straw.

Straw is one of the fastest materials to build with. A skilled team of straw-bale builders can construct a basic house in just a few days. Straw is also a waste product from farming, so it is cheap and makes use of a material that might otherwise just be destroyed. Straw bales also offer good insulation once the house is built, which can dramatically reduce the need for heating in a finished home. They are also very soundproof.

Earth can be used to build walls using a process known as "rammed-earth." The earth is mixed with sand and clay and is used to fill in gaps in a wooden framework to make walls. The mixture is "rammed" by hand or by machine until it is solid and strong,

and then the framework can be removed, leaving a sturdy structure. Although rammed-earth walls are not as efficient insulators as straw-bale walls, they heat up slowly during the day and release that heat throughout the evening. Earth as a building material is widely available.

EXPERT VIEW

"In the West, mud is effectively regarded as dirt, yet in rural Africa (as in so much of the world), it is the most common of building materials with which everybody has direct contact. Maintaining and resurfacing of buildings is part of the rhythm of life, and there is an ongoing and active participation in their continuing existence."
JAMES MORRIS, *THE ARCHITECTURAL REVIEW*, 2004

The cost of straw can be 15 times less than that of bricks. The straw bales can be seen making up the walls here —they will eventually be covered with plaster or concrete render, and the house will look like any other.

In rural areas of LEDCs, both straw and earth are commonly used as building materials, and the houses are completely sustainable. They are becoming increasingly popular in MEDCs as people appreciate their environmental benefits, but materials like earth and straw are still not widely used in wealthier nations. So why are man-made building materials still so popular?

Traditional or Man-Made Materials?

One of the main problems with natural materials like earth and straw is that they are not ideal for use everywhere. Usually, straw-bale and rammed-earth houses are built in rural areas, where the materials are more readily available and do not have to be transported long distances. They are also best built in dry areas rather than countries where there is a lot of rainfall. Although earth and straw houses can be protected against rain by covering the outside with plaster, they are still more susceptible to rain and damp than houses built with materials such as brick and concrete.

The walls must be kept in good condition and continually repaired and maintained.

Another problem with sustainable building materials is linked to labor. Building rammed-earth and straw-bale houses is more labor-intensive than using less sustainable materials. In countries like Africa or the Middle East, labor is cheap, so it is more practical to build these kinds of houses there than it is in MEDCs, where building specialists can charge a lot more.

Roofing Materials

It is not just walls that can be made in a more environmentally friendly way. Roofs can also be made from more sustainable materials than concrete or clay tiles. Slate, for example, is a natural roofing material that is readily available in many countries. Other materials, including cedar and oak, are alternatives to concrete or clay. Although wood is not completely sustainable—gaining the timber can harm the environment—it takes less energy to produce it.

Rammed-earth housing is a feature of the Middle Eastern country of Yemen. In dry countries and places where labor is cheap, rammed-earth building is a sustainable solution to the housing problem.

Living roofs on houses in the Faroe Islands in Denmark. Roofing houses with soil and vegetation is becoming increasingly popular in countries like the United States, but it has been practiced in Scandinavia for many years.

Living Roofs

"Living" roofs are made of plants (normally grasses) that have been planted in a thin layer of soil. Like many natural materials, using soil and vegetation for roofing is not a new idea—"sod roofs" have been used on traditional houses in Scandinavia for centuries—but in the past few years, it has gained popularity in other parts of the world. Germany has led the way in developing living-roof technology, and it is now big business there—around 10 percent of roofs in Germany have been "greened."

There are different types of green roofs. Some, like the traditional Scandinavian ones, are "pitched," which means they slope downward. Other living roofs are flat, so people can use them as a kind of garden. These are especially good in built-up areas, where outside space is limited.

Living roofs have a number of benefits. Reports suggest that they reduce heat loss, which saves energy. They make good sound insulation, they reduce stormwater runoff by absorbing the water into the soil, and they help filter pollutants out of rainwater. Different kinds of vegetation can be used, and this can provide a habitat for birds and insects.

One of the drawbacks of living roofs is that they can be more expensive than ordinary roofs. They require maintenance to ensure that growth is controlled and that unwanted vegetation does not take root. It is not always possible to fit an existing house with a new green roof because the soil and vegetation can be quite heavy, and the house structure might not be able to support it. The house must also have good waterproofing, which can be expensive to install.

Sustainable Houses in LEDCs

Many people in MEDCs are taking traditional building materials and using modern technologies to create sustainable homes. But such technologies can be expensive, and they are often only available to people who live in wealthier countries. So how are people in less developed countries working toward more sustainable homes?

The same natural materials—earth, straw, wood—are often readily available in LEDCs, and they have been used for many years to build homes. One of the problems, though, lies in creating strong, long-lasting houses, rather than just temporary shelters. In recent years, low-cost housing—constructed to meet the needs of rapid population growth in some of the poorest parts of the world—has been built using materials like corrugated metal, which makes it cheap to buy and quick to build. Such houses are unsustainable and provide a poor quality of life.

There are many programs under way in LEDCs—notably in Africa and South America, to establish sustainable "ecohousing." The village of Thlolego in South Africa is an example of this. The inhabitants were trained in sustainable building technologies so they could help build their own "eco-friendly" homes. They used locally

FACTS IN FOCUS
Start Simple

In LEDCs, there are simple actions that can be taken to make buildings more sustainable. These include using local materials such as earth bricks. Many low-income buildings are built without ceilings and instead have a roof built straight on top of the walls. Adding a ceiling is a relatively low-cost measure, but trapping a layer of air (between the ceiling and the roof) helps prevent the room from becoming too hot in summer or too cold in winter. In South Africa, adding ceilings to existing houses has reduced energy use by more than 50 percent.

sourced, natural materials to reduce the impact on the environment and included modern ideas such as passive solar design (positioning the house to make the most of the sun's light and heat).

Residents of Thlolego help to build their own sustainable home, which saves on the cost of labor.

Sustainable Designs

Choosing to use natural, locally sourced materials is important in planning a sustainable home, but there are other considerations, too. The passive solar design of the houses in Thlolego and the Earthships in parts of the United States and elsewhere (see Case Study below) is one example of this. Design and planning play key roles in making a house truly sustainable. Detailed planning—such as designing an earth cellar to store food, keeping it cool naturally rather than using a refrigerator, for example—can make sure a home is sustainable from the ground up.

The size of the home plays a part, too. Large houses cost a lot to build, use up resources, and consume a lot of energy during the construction process. They are also not very energy efficient once they have been completed, so they cost more to run. The best sustainable homes are just the right size to fit comfortably the number of people who live there, because acceptable standards of living are an important part of sustainability. Once again, planning for efficient use of space within the home, considering how possessions can be stored, and thinking about how each room will be used are all part of sustainable design.

CASE STUDY

United States: Earthships

Earthships are passive solar homes—designed to make the best use of heat from the sun to improve "thermal mass" (the way a house stores heat)—made by the American company Earthship Biotecture. They are made of natural and recyclable materials and generally use resources that are available locally. The outside walls are built from car tires filled with earth. These "bricks" are extremely strong, fire-resistant, and, most important, are good thermal insulators. Inside walls are often made from recycled aluminum cans, connected using concrete in a sort of honeycomb. Windows are positioned to maximize sunlight in the house. Earthships have been so successful in the United States that several LEDCs, including Mexico and Bolivia, are starting to build them.

The outside of this Earthship has been painted, but the bulges of the tires that make the outer walls can be seen.

BoKlok houses have proven to be a solution to the problem of affordable housing in Scandinavia, where around 1,000 are built every year.

BoKlok

Building a sustainable home is not always cheap, and a number of organizations have started investigating ways of building more affordable sustainable homes that mean more people can make environmentally friendly choices. One of the most successful of these projects has been BoKlok.

BoKlok—which means "live smart"—was created by the furniture company IKEA and the Swedish construction company Skanska. They developed a house system in which the pieces that make up the structure of a home are manufactured in factories rather than built, and then assembled on site. This kind of "flat-pack" housing means that waste is limited, and the pollution and energy used in transportation of materials is dramatically reduced. Natural construction materials help to reduce energy use, and each home includes solar panels and low-energy heating. The interior of a BoKlok house is designed as an open-plan living space, which makes it feel spacious. The windows are large, so they make the most of natural light rather than relying on electric lighting.

BoKlok homes come as apartments or townhouses, and there are several developments made up of this type of house in Scandinavia. Other countries have also realized the benefits of this sustainable building practice and have plans for their own BoKlok-style complexes, including one in Gateshead in the United Kingdom. The sustainable nature of the BoKlok houses extends outside the buildings, too. For example, parking is kept to a minimum in these areas to encourage people to use more sustainable transportation systems, and playgrounds are included to provide livable community spaces.

Energy in the Home

Constructing a sustainable home involves selecting the right materials and designing a space that meets the needs of the people who will be using it—whether they live in a city in an MEDC or a rural village in an LEDC. But the sustainability of homes does not end once they have been built. An important part of planning an environmentally friendly home is considering energy use for the lifetime of the property. Building an energy-efficient home saves on precious natural resources and can save the owners a lot of money in the long run.

Energy and the Environment

There are simply not enough resources to continue building homes as we have been for the past century, but there is an increasing demand for homes that mirrors the growth in the world population. As experts realized the impact on the environment of building and energy use in the home, they began to consider ways of limiting this impact. This is important because a lot of the energy we use comes from limited resources, and obtaining it can cause serious environmental damage. Fossil fuels like coal—which are used to create electricity to power homes—are running out. These and other resources, such as minerals used to make concrete, have to be mined, which destroys habitats for plants and animals. Architects, designers, and environmental groups realized that reducing energy in housing was not just about the materials and construction methods used. It also meant building homes that require less energy to run.

Simple and Grand Designs

Architects and planners have come up with many ideas for houses that can be built with energy saving in mind. Some of these plans can be quite simple, such as the idea of "upside-down" houses.

This ecohome in the United Kingdom uses a lot of glass, solar panels, and cutting-edge insulation. It can save about $1,000 per year on fuel bills.

These are designed so that the main living areas are on the upper floors and the rooms that are used less, such as bedrooms, are on the lower ones. Because heat rises, the upper floors are warmer than the lower ones, so energy can be saved on heating.

Other simple energy-saving designs include making the surface area of the house as low as possible so that less heat is lost through outside walls, incorporating good insulation into the planning, and making use of natural ventilation. Using a lot of glass can also help, as it allows natural light to flood into a house, reducing the amount of electricity needed to light a home.

Architects have also come up with some more dramatic designs for energy-saving homes. They may be unusual shapes—domes make for energy-efficient homes, for example. In fact, a special type of housing called "geodesic domes" is often used to provide emergency housing in LEDCs because the buildings are inexpensive and quick to construct, as well. In MEDCs, the design has been adapted to create modern, energy-efficient homes for wealthier people.

EXPERT VIEW

"While the environmental and human health benefits of green building have been widely recognized . . . increases in up-front costs of 0–2 percent to support green design will result in life cycle savings of 20 percent."
FROM "THE COSTS AND BENEFITS OF GREEN BUILDINGS"

Dome-shaped houses are energy-efficient because they have a smaller surface area than traditionally shaped houses. This means that less heat is lost through the walls.

Low-Impact Housing

Architects and planners are now making energy saving a priority when designing new housing. Even where homes do not make use of more natural and sustainable building materials, they can still lower their impact on the environment. This is important because many countries, especially MEDCs, already have a lot of houses and cannot afford to rebuild every home to make it sustainable. How can existing homes be adapted to make them more sustainable and energy efficient?

There are a number of ways that homes can be modified to reduce their energy use by generating their own power supply, for example. Solar panels in particular are one of the most efficient ways of using a renewable resource to generate energy in the homes. They are a clever design that integrates photovoltaic (PV) cells or solar thermal energy (for heating water) into the actual roofing material. The system is fitted just like normal roofing tiles and looks very similar, too, so people do not mind them on their homes. When fitted to a family home typical of those found in MEDCs, solar panels can reduce bills by more than 60 percent. There are plans now in many countries to help people install these panels on the roofs of their houses as part of the drive toward converting existing buildings into more sustainable homes (see Case Study below).

CASE STUDY

United States: Solar Roofs

In 2006, the Million Solar Roofs Initiative was launched in California. This is a plan to reduce the reliance on valuable fossil fuels for generating electricity and instead encourage people to install solar panels on the roofs of domestic houses. California is an ideal location for harnessing solar energy because of the high levels of sunlight it receives. In the first year alone, the initiative nearly doubled the amount of solar power used in the area, reducing the impact on the environment and cutting energy costs for homeowners. The governor of California, Arnold Schwarzenegger, said: "My Million Solar Roofs Plan will provide 3,000 megawatts of additional clean energy and reduce the output of greenhouse gases by three million tons, which is like taking one million cars off the road."

In California, where sunlight is plentiful, solar panels are an ideal alternative to fossil fuels for providing energy in the home.

Proper insulation in walls and ceilings can improve an existing home's energy efficiency.

Around half the heat used in a typical home is lost through the roof and walls. Insulating these areas—by packing the spaces between them with special materials to prevent heat loss—is a relatively cheap process. This can be done using natural materials such as sheep's wool or cellulose (made from recycled paper). Insulating hot water pipes, blocking drafts, and installing double-glazed windows also help to reduce energy use and costs.

Water is another key area where improvements can be made in all homes. Low- or dual-flush toilets, for example, can reduce the water used for flushing by up to 80 percent. Low-volume showers can offer similar savings in water use. Both technologies are available at a relatively low cost.

Making It Easy

To allow individuals to make sustainable choices, it must be simple and affordable to adopt solutions such as installing solar panels on the roof of a house or having a wind turbine in a garden to generate electricity from renewable resources. Until recently, it was expensive and difficult to install such technologies on private houses in the United States. But in recent years, with energy efficiency becoming a bigger priority, the government is looking for ways to use this technology more widely.

FACTS IN FOCUS
Can We Afford It?

It might seem that sustainable technologies cost more than less sustainable solutions. People often only think about the "off the shelf" price—how much something is going to cost to buy and install. However, there are other costs that must also be considered, not just money. There is the cost to the environment and the cost to health, for example. There is also the "payback period" to think about. This is the time it takes for a product to pay for itself in cost savings. An energy-saving lightbulb might cost more than a standard one, but it lasts 10 to 12 times longer and uses up to 80 percent less electricity. The "payback period" for an energy-saving lightbulb is four to six months.

Energy-saving lightbulbs are more expensive to buy, but more than pay for themselves in energy savings.

The Cost of Sustainability

One of the biggest complaints about sustainable technologies is how much they cost. Many people would like to use them, but simply can't afford to. Technologies like solar panels seem expensive to buy and install, so many people think it is cheaper to use traditional energy sources, even if they are worse for the environment. In fact, the reduction in fuel bills over the lifetime of a solar panel is significant. In the long run, it is actually cheaper to install solar panels. This is known as "real" cost, and it can often save households a lot of money. Sustainable planning like this has long-term benefits. For this reason, governments around the world are finding ways of making it easier for people to invest in sustainable technologies. They have come up with a range of incentives.

Incentive Policies

Among the most successful incentive policies are "renewable energy payments." This means that people who generate their own energy using renewable sources, such as wind or solar power, can sell any extra energy to energy suppliers for a guaranteed price.

One of the most successful renewable energy payment policies was established in Germany. Here, a renewable energy payment four times the current market rate for electricity was agreed upon in 1999 and guaranteed for 20 years. This means a solar panel can pay for itself in less than 10 years and can make extra money for the owner after that, when the excess energy is sold to national energy suppliers. Farmers have become big customers for solar panels in Germany, because they can convert large barn roofs into solar farms. All renewable energy types qualify for the payment, and now 12 percent of Germany's electricity comes from renewable sources. Around 50 other countries are in the process of starting similar plans. These include countries like Spain and Denmark, but also less developed countries such as China.

Opting for a private wind turbine to generate electricity is now a viable option for many people.

EXPERT VIEW

"The general target is to mobilize all renewable options, producing a renewable energy mix and reducing the dependency on conventional energy over time."
HERMANN SCHEER, GERMAN RENEWABLE ENERGY PIONEER

A Helping Hand

Incentive plans can encourage wealthier people to invest in sustainable technology, but for poorer people, this may not be an option. Offering more direct help is another way that governments can encourage sustainability. In Japan, for example, the government launched a 10-year "million solar roofs" plan in 1994 by providing subsidies to help people pay for solar panels. By paying for half of the cost of all new systems, the government improved the market for solar panels in Japan. By 2005, the cost of a residential solar system in Japan had fallen by 72 percent. This meant that the government could then stop paying the subsidy because people could afford the technology without help. The Californian plan (see page 22) used the Japanese one as an example.

TAKE ACTION

- Switch off lights and appliances when you're not using them. Standby mode still uses energy!
- Use energy-efficient lightbulbs wherever you can.
- Use an energy provider that is investing in renewable energy.
- Only use as much water as you need in a sink or tub, rather than filling it up.
- Put on a sweater or open a window rather than adjusting the heating or air conditioning.
- Improve the insulation of your home—there may be grants available.

Members of an environmental group campaign for solar panels in Japan. In Tokyo, a successful plan has seen a dramatic rise in the use of solar energy.

Sustainable Communities

Planning and building individual sustainable homes is one element of a bigger plan to solve the global housing crisis and to develop the building industry in an environmentally friendly way. For homes to be truly sustainable, they must be part of whole communities that are also planned around sustainability. To achieve this, experts are looking not only at housing, but also at land use and infrastructures such as transportation systems and waste management.

Effective Use of Land

Land use is one of the most important considerations when planning a sustainable community. The cost and availability of land will affect the kind of housing that can be built on it. In big cities, not much land is available, so making the best use of it—by planning high-density housing, for example (see pages 36–37)—can make a big difference.

Planning high-rise housing can reduce costs. This is especially important in less economically developed countries, where more people are on low incomes. Many of these countries have the fastest-growing populations and therefore the most urgent need for housing solutions. Providing services for people concentrated into a small area is also more cost-effective than more spread-out housing. There is less need for roads, pipelines, wiring, and other infrastructures that would be needed to connect housing that was dispersed more widely. Such solutions can address the big problem of urban sprawl (see page 9), where suburban houses often have to be independently

Refurbished high-rise apartments in Berlin, Germany, have been fitted with solar panels to provide a renewable source of energy for their inhabitants.

The Docklands development in the East End of London was built on a brownfield site—former industrial land that was lying idle. Revitalizing areas like this is sustainable as it does not require rural land to be developed.

connected to basic services, and people are dependent on private cars to commute to their jobs in the city centers.

Brownfield Sites

Many cities have areas of industrial land that now lie abandoned or vacant. These so-called "brownfield" sites provide an ideal opportunity to begin redeveloping cities more sustainably. Planners call this "urban regeneration." Careful planning about what is built, who will use it, and how it is connected to the rest of the city can all deliver successful and highly sustainable projects such as the Jätkäsaari suburb of Helsinki, Finland (see page 32).

Many countries are now using brownfield sites for housing development, because it reduces the impact on the environment—instead of cities spreading out into surrounding rural areas, land is being redeveloped and reused. An example of this

is the Docklands area of East London, which was run-down, wasted land. Housing built with sustainability in mind, shops, and transportation systems have all been incorporated into a now-thriving sustainable settlement here. All across MEDCs there are brownfield sites that could be—and are being—developed in a similar way. In the United States alone, there are more than 450,000 brownfield sites that could be made use of.

EXPERT VIEW

"How can we build more housing and at the same time give the city a better shape? How can the amount of housing units be increased while expanding public space? . . . The resources invested in real estate can be linked to the creation of open spaces . . . to achieve forms of development that are sustainable."
JAVIER SÁNCHEZ, ARCHITECT

Smart Growth

Reusing existing land is one way of developing sustainable communities. Another is to reuse existing buildings. In MEDCs in particular, governments are considering ways of addressing the problems of urbanization and using its potential for regenerating areas in already large cities. Smart Growth is an urban planning program in the United States that concentrates housing and transportation in city centers. Its aim is to reduce urban sprawl and focus on revitalizing existing centers and infrastructures. One of Smart Growth's main principles is to provide quality housing for everyone—no matter what their income. It believes that a range of housing should be made available, but instead of new developments in outer areas, existing buildings should be converted to provide accommodation. For example, an old hospital in the New York borough of Brooklyn was converted into apartments for women and children, who made up a majority of people in low-cost housing in the area. This is just one of many ways of developing urban areas sustainably and offering better-quality homes to people who could not otherwise afford them.

Getting Around

The success of Curitiba's sustainable transportation system (see page 10) was based on careful thinking about the structure and order of the city. Other communities are now following this example and beginning to think about basic infrastructure

Water transportation in places like Istanbul, Turkey, offers a good alternative to private car use.

Barcelona's "Bicing" program is computerized, so people can find out where the nearest available bicycle is before they leave home.

(transportation, energy, water, and waste systems). In rural settlements, private vehicles can be an essential part of people's mobility because the population is too small to support a regular public transportation system. In places where more people live, public transportation options, including buses, taxis, trams, and railways, all become more realistic choices. Many city authorities are encouraging greater use of public transportation by investing in systems that allow people to use all forms of transportation with a single ticket.

Walking and bicycling are even more sustainable choices. People sometimes avoid walking or bicycling because of fears about safety. Providing dedicated bicycle and pedestrian paths and street lighting can help. In Barcelona, Spain, a community bicycle network called "Bicing" was started in 2007, with more than 1,500 bicycles distributed between 100 collection points throughout the city. Members can collect a bicycle from any point and use it free for journeys of less than 30 minutes, dropping it off at a point close to their destination.

FACTS IN FOCUS

Waste Management

Waste management is another area where city planners are thinking more sustainably. In many lower-income countries, waste is treated as a resource and is actively collected, processed, and reused or recycled. This process could be copied on a larger scale across the world. Kalundborg in Denmark is a good example of how the process works. Since the 1970s, industries in Kalundborg have cooperated to use each others' waste as a resource or raw material for another activity. Around 3.3 million tons (3 million t) of material are exchanged each year, including waste steam from a power station that is used in a district heating system for more than 20,000 residents.

The Hammarby development is due to be completed in 2015. Around 20,000 people will live there and another 10,000 will travel to work there.

Hammarby Sjöstad

One of the best examples of a sustainable settlement is Hammarby Sjöstad in Stockholm, Sweden. This is not just a suburb—it is a whole city district. Built on a brownfield site on the edge of a lake, everything about Hammarby is designed to be sustainable. Although the houses are of different shapes and sizes, they are made of natural, recyclable materials, which means the building process uses less energy and water. The district has its own waste management, energy generation, and water treatment systems. It connects directly to Stockholm's public transportation system, encouraging people to use their cars less, which is better for the environment.

There are already people living in Hammarby, and the benefits are showing. A survey of residents in 2005 found that although similar numbers of people there owned cars compared with the rest of Stockholm, two-thirds of all journeys were made by public transportation, by bicycle, or on foot. Eight percent of residents had joined a carpool. An important part of the Hammarby development is an environmental education center (called the Glasshouse), which gives residents advice on how they can live more sustainably.

Meeting Needs

Hammarby Sjöstad and Freiburg, Germany (see Case Study below), are good examples of how sustainable planning can work on a large scale. However, it is important to remember that they can be very expensive, and this is passed on in the cost of buying a house in these areas. Hammarby Sjöstad has been criticized by some for not providing more affordable housing for people with lower incomes.

In many countries, the technology used in places like Hammarby is simply too expensive, but there are ways in which communities can be made more sustainable. In Mexico City, Mexico, the Proaire Initiative is installing energy-efficient lightbulbs in 30,000 new homes and 45,000 existing homes. These will reduce energy use, but Mexico City is also taking action to generate its own energy, with plans to install solar heating systems on at least 50,000 homes.

Similar initiatives are being introduced in other LEDCs, too. In China, around 40 million homes had solar water heaters in 2007, which saves the equivalent of 16.5 millon tons (15 million t) of carbon dioxide every year. India is investing in wind power to meet the needs of its fast-growing population. By 2007, India had become the fourth biggest wind power producer in the world.

CASE STUDY

Germany: Freiburg

Freiburg is a good example of how a community can prosper and still be sustainable. Since the mid-1980s, this city of around 200,000 people has placed sustainable development at the heart of all its planning in energy, transportation, housing, waste, and industry. All new houses must meet design standards that conform to particular energy limits. This increases building costs, but reduces energy costs and carbon dioxide emissions. More than 300 miles (500 km) of bicycle paths and parking for more than 5,000 bicycles has led to a third of all journeys in Freiburg being made by bicycle. This and a new tram system introduced in 2004 have led to 35 percent of residents choosing not to own a car at all.

Bicycle lanes and buildings with solar and photovoltaic cells have made Freiburg an example of how sustainable planning can be applied to whole communities.

The Cities of Tomorrow

There are many examples of smaller sustainable communities, but how can the policies of sustainable development be applied to whole cities in the future? In cities such as Karachi in Pakistan or Nairobi in Kenya, poor-quality housing can appear literally overnight, so as urbanization increases, governments and planners must meet the challenge of providing high-quality, sustainable housing in large urban areas.

Ecocities

Ecocities are cities that are completely planned around sustainability and the environment. Not long ago, being able to create a whole city in this way was just a dream, but now there are several projects turning it into a reality. Such plans are starting small, but experts hope they will grow. Just outside Helsinki in Finland, for example, the whole suburb of Jätkäsaari is a car-free zone. When completed, around 15,000 people will live in an area free from traffic pollution. It is an environmentally friendly development that has been designed to reflect its natural surroundings.

In the Republic of Ireland, sustainable activities are being encouraged in a suburb on the outskirts of Dublin. Authorities have implemented laws that mean heating and electricity in homes must come from renewable resources, and building materials must also be sustainable and recyclable. If plans like this prove successful in the suburbs, they could be applied to the cities themselves, offering large-scale sustainable solutions.

Newington Suburb

Newington is a suburb in Sydney, Australia. There are 2,000 homes there, and they have all been designed with sustainability in mind.

Newington was home to the Athlete's Village for the 2000 Olympics, and this development encouraged the sustainable planning of the suburb. The Village itself made use of solar panels.

EXPERT VIEW

"We are realistic enough to know that many Jätkäsaari residents will want their own wheels, but our idea is that local services and routes will be planned so that a car will not be needed for local access."
MATTI KAIJANSINKKO, JÄTKÄSAARI PROJECT LEADER, 2007

When planning the 2008 Beijing Olympics, sustainability was a key factor. Buildings were designed with energy efficiency in mind, and efforts were made to reduce the environmental impact. Despite this, the development was very controversial because thousands of people were evicted from their homes to make way for it.

Each home is positioned to make the best use of sunlight, and they all have special insulation that means heat loss is dramatically reduced, cutting energy costs. Solar panels provide hot water and electricity to every house, and a dual-pipe water system provides recycled water for flushing toilets or watering gardens. There is a network of bicycle paths and public footpaths, which encourages people to bicycle or walk rather than use cars. These both have connections to Sydney's local transportation network, so commuting from Newington into downtown Sydney is easy.

The people who live in Newington have found their energy bills are a lot less than in other places they have lived. The developers estimate that each home uses around half the energy of similar homes in other parts of the city. According to Greenpeace Australia, the energy saved by the Newington suburb reduces emissions of carbon dioxide by about 2,756 tons (2,500 t) per year.

This is the same as removing 2,500 cars with an annual mileage of 6,200 miles (10,000 km) each from the roads every year.

The Beijing Olympic Village

Before the Olympics in Beijing in 2008, planners took the example of Newington and looked at ways of making their own Olympic Village as sustainable as possible. The finished settlement was the largest "green" neighborhood in the world. Buildings were designed to reduce energy use by using cutting-edge insulation, energy-efficient windows, and solar roofs. Such planning was particularly important in China. Beijing is a large city that suffers especially from air pollution caused by traffic. The Olympic development was part of plans for a long-term sustainable future for the city. The houses in the Olympic Village were sold off as commercial properties after the Games, and the large green was made available for public use.

Visitors view a model of the ecocity Masdar at the World Future Energy Summit in Abu Dhabi in 2008. Masdar has been designed as a zero-carbon, zero-waste city of the future.

Masdar City

On a larger scale, there are plans for completely new ecocities that can house tens of thousands of people. In Abu Dhabi, a new zero-carbon, zero-waste city called Masdar City welcomed the first of around 50,000 new residents during 2009. The developers claim the city will use 75 percent less energy and 40 percent less water than existing communities. The city will be powered entirely by solar energy and other renewable resources. A large solar power plant converts solar energy into electricity for homes for 50,000 people. Solar cells are also incorporated into the design of individual houses. There are also plans to build the world's largest hydrogen power plant at Masdar, furthering its use of renewable resources. The city will be a car-free zone, and public transportation will be provided by special systems called personal rapid transit systems. These are small, independent "pods" that run on dedicated roads and rails. Without relying on fossil fuels for energy and transportation fuel, the designers of Masdar City hope that it will eventually have no carbon emissions at all.

Another sustainable plan for Masdar is reducing waste to zero. This will be accomplished by reusing biological waste as a fertilizer for gardens and public spaces. Incinerating (burning) other waste will provide an alternative power source.

Dongtan

Dongtan ecocity in China follows similar principles as Masdar but is even larger—there may be as many as half a million people living there by 2030. This makes it by far the world's largest planned sustainable community, and many see Dongtan as the example that other countries should be following. Not everyone agrees, though. Some people are concerned that Dongtan and Masdar might only attract the wealthiest people. Others think that it might take too long to develop these communities in a truly sustainable way.

Systems of personal rapid transit pods like this one are being included in the plans for ecocities all over the world.

CASE STUDY

Canada: Dockside Green

Dockside Green, in Victoria, Canada, is an environmentally friendly development being built near Victoria Harbour. It will have a special plant that converts wood chips into a gas that will supply energy to the community. It will also have its own sewage treatment plant and public transportation system that will discourage car use. Most important, it is being designed so that people of all different income levels will be able to live there. Housing for people with lower incomes is being built as part of the first phase of the development.

This artist's impression of Dockside Green shows its design around the principles of "green architecture." Homes there will be available to people at all different levels of income—not just the wealthiest.

Housing in the Cities of the Future

For all the grand plans for environmentally friendly developments in energy supply, transportation, and other infrastructures, housing remains at the heart of truly sustainable development. Providing suitable housing for increasing numbers of people in urban areas is a big challenge, but the cities of the future can draw some lessons from ideas that have already been implemented in large cities around the world. In particular, one of the key solutions to the housing crisis might be building more high-density housing.

High-Density Housing

High-density housing is made up of high-rise apartment buildings or houses built close together, to accommodate large numbers of people. It is intended to be affordable for people on low incomes, which is particularly important in LEDCs, where urbanization is occurring more rapidly than elsewhere. Often, people moving to the cities cannot afford to buy or rent properties in the city centers.

High-density housing offers several advantages over individual detached houses. Where houses or apartments are joined, there are fewer external walls, and this can greatly reduce energy loss. The costs of sustainable technology such as solar panels or solar heating can also be shared and made more affordable. In Los Angeles and Berlin, several apartment buildings are now covered with solar panels to provide electricity for their residents in this sort of shared concept (see page 26). Similar advantages can be made in water management, with rain harvesting and the treatment and recycling of wastewater.

CASE STUDY

Hong Kong: Wah Fu

There are many high-rise buildings in Hong Kong because of the number of people who live and work there, but property prices are among the highest in the world. Wah Fu is a high-density development built in 1967 in an attempt to solve the housing crisis, and to improve living conditions for people who were then living in slums or tenement buildings. It is now home to 57,000 people. The density of Wah Fu means it can support its own community and reduce the need for its residents to travel. It has amenities such as its own market, shopping center, restaurants, public library, and primary and secondary schools. The low rents mean that even people with lower incomes can afford a decent standard of living.

High-density housing has become a sustainable solution to the housing problems in Hong Kong.

High-density housing stands next to the Docklands Light Railway that takes workers into the city. The Docklands development included addressing the problem of poor-quality and insufficient housing in London.

High-density and high-rise housing is not a new idea, and examples can be found in many parts of the world, not just cities like Berlin or Los Angeles. In Hong Kong, for example, high-density apartments have long been used to solve problems of overcrowding and to improve living conditions (see Case Study opposite).

EXPERT VIEW

"We grow vegetables, we grow plants. A lot of people come here and really enjoy the process. People make friends, it helps build a better community. It's also a much healthier lifestyle for people here."
ANGUS LEE, RESIDENT OF WAH FU

The Problems with High-Rises

High-rise buildings are not the solution everywhere. In countries where earthquakes are common, for example, high-rise buildings can be extremely dangerous—causing more damage and death if they collapse than occurs with smaller structures. Pakistan is an example of this. Population numbers are high in this relatively poor nation, so urgent solutions are needed for the housing crisis. But the country is prone to earthquakes, so planning sustainable homes has to go beyond energy saving and consider earthquake safety as a priority. After an earthquake in 2005, international organizations began working with carpenters in Pakistan to help them design and build strong timber-frame homes that would withstand earthquakes.

Public Buildings

Homes are the heart of any community, but there are other buildings that play a big role in communities, including schools, offices, hospitals, factories, and shops. These are often large buildings that are used by lots of people. As a result, they use a lot of energy, water, and other resources. Making public buildings more sustainable could reduce the use of limited resources and set an example of how whole communities can be developed without damage.

Already, governments and other organizations have begun making public buildings more sustainable. In Germany, for example, the Reichstag (government building) in Berlin was redeveloped after a fire destroyed the old building. It was planned to be a completely sustainable public building. Renewable fuels such as vegetable oil are used to generate energy, which reduces the carbon emissions caused by traditional fuels. Any heat that is not needed by the building is stored in an aquifer beneath the building. During the winter, warm water is pumped up from the aquifer to heat the Reichstag. The building works as a local power plant, supplying energy to other nearby government buildings.

City Hall, the headquarters of the London Assembly in England, has also been designed along similarly sustainable lines. The building's bulbous shape reduces surface area, which limits heat loss, and its use of glass allows in lots of natural light. There are also plans to add solar cells to the building, enhancing its energy efficiency.

EXPERT VIEW

"The building's energy strategy is radical. It uses renewable biofuel—refined vegetable oil—which when burned . . . is far cleaner than fossil fuels. The result is a 94 percent reduction in carbon dioxide emissions."

FOSTER + PARTNERS, ARCHITECTS OF THE REICHSTAG

The dome of the Reichstag building in Berlin contains a cone made of mirrors. This directs sunlight into the building below, making the most of natural light.

In Tokyo, "green spaces"—areas of gardens and parks—are included in the plans for all building development.

Green Spaces

Thinking about the quality of life of people who live in urban areas has become an important part of city planning. Large cities in both LEDCs and MEDCs often have high levels of air pollution; they can be dirty and run-down. People do not have large yards, and often they have no outside space at all. This can have a detrimental effect on mental and physical well-being.

It seems that there is no turning the tide of urbanization, so to address the needs of people living in cities that go beyond simply providing somewhere to live, planners have implemented plans that provide "green spaces" for people to enjoy in the hearts of cities. Several governments have even changed their laws to enforce much stricter controls on the amount of public space that must be made available in cities. In Tokyo, for example, any building development over 3,281 square feet (1,000 sq m) in area must include green gardens on at least 20 percent of its roofing area. These green roofs help to absorb the heat from the city and also take in carbon dioxide, which might otherwise be released into the atmosphere and contribute to global warming. School yards are also being "greened" and have helped reduce temperatures across the city.

PlaNYC

Another example of forward planning is PlaNYC. This is a program to make New York a more sustainable city. Among many initiatives included in this is a plan to build housing for more than a million new residents and to make housing more affordable and sustainable. The planners have also included a "10-minute rule," which means that when implemented, residents of New York will all be within 10 minutes' walk of a park. It is likely that more and more cities will adopt similar plans for sustainable development in the future.

Global Housing Solutions

What will the settlements of 2050 look like? Will we be traveling around in pods like those planned for Masdar City? Will our waste disappear into vast automated systems underground like those in Hammarby Sjöstad? Will concrete be a building material from the past, and will the idea of individual homes and yards be considered an extravagant idea from history?

Get Real!

In reality, 2050 is not that far away, and things will probably not look that different in many communities than they do today. After all, many of the newest and most challenging sustainable communities will only recently have been completed. There is also the very real issue of a fast-growing population and the continuing move of people into urban areas. There are already slums of more than a million people in countries like Kenya and India. The need to improve these most basic of housing needs is already a priority.

Seize the Opportunity

The development opportunities that arise can be used to make long-term, sustainable decisions. In slum-improvement projects, for example, positioning houses to benefit from the warmth of the sun is a sustainable option that costs nothing. Adapting the design of existing basic shelters so they are better insulated (by fitting a ceiling, for example) is another intelligent response, and using local materials could provide jobs, too. Energy choices can also be made in such plans. It is relatively easy to collect sewage and organic waste from homes and convert it into biogas for cooking and heating. This in turn reduces the use of wood and charcoal—major causes of air pollution.

Children play in front of traditional but sustainably built huts in the ecovillage of Mognori in Ghana.

It is predicted that by 2030, around 35 percent of houses around the world will be newly built. In countries with faster-growing populations, the proportion will be even higher.

Global Sustainability

Our planet and its resources cannot meet the needs of the growing world population and support the building industry at its current rate, so more sustainable housing and communities must be a key part of a global development plan. Many people who support the development of sustainable houses think that we should not be focusing on the expensive technology that might only be available in MEDCs. Instead, they point to the many simple solutions that could contribute to a more sustainable future all over the world.

Success stories like Curitiba (see page 10) and programs like Smart Growth (see page 28) are just two examples of how sustainable development can work in communities in both developed and developing nations. Countries can learn from one another. Often, LEDCs have valuable lessons to teach MEDCs—the pressure for finding housing solutions can be greater in poorer countries, so it is

EXPERT VIEW

''The car you buy, the house you live in, the lifestyle you follow, the choices you make, will all play a major role in deciding the fate of the planet.''
EUROPEAN COMMISSION, DIRECTORATE-GENERAL FOR ENERGY AND TRANSPORT, 2008

a higher priority than in wealthier ones.

Governments and organizations all over the world are working on sharing information on housing solutions. Solutions that work in one place may not be effective in another, but often ideas can be adapted. Help can even be offered. Educating people is a key factor in the long-term success of these ideas. As people understand the problems and the range of solutions, our homes and communities will begin to contribute significantly to a sustainable future.

facts and figures

World Population Growth (1950–2050)

Year	Population (thousands)
1950	2,535,093
1960	3,031,931
1970	3,698,676
1980	4,451,470
1990	5,294,879
2000	6,124,123
2010*	6,906,558
2020*	7,667,090
2030*	8,317,707
2040*	8,823,546
2050*	9,075,900

* Estimated
Source: United Nations Population Fund 2007

Largest Cities in the World (2008)

City	Population
Tokyo (Japan)	33,800,000
Seoul (South Korea)	23,800,000
Mexico City (Mexico)	22,800,000
Mumbai (India)	22,200,000
Delhi (India)	22,200,000
New York (USA)	21,900,000
São Paulo (Brazil)	20,900,000
Manila (Philippines)	19,000,000
Los Angeles (USA)	18,000,000
Shanghai (China)	17,900,000

Source: Thomas Brinkhoff: The Principal Agglomerations of the World, http://www.citypopulation.de, 9/14/2008

Global Slum Population by Region

Region	% Slum Population
South Asia	27.7
Africa	22.1
China	19.6
Latin America and the Caribbean	13.5
Other Asia	11.0
Rest of the world	6.1

Source: UN-HABITAT, State of the World's Cities 2006/07

Slum Facts

- More than 90 percent of slums and shantytowns are in LEDCs.
- In many sub-Saharan African cities, more than 70 percent of the urban population lives in slums.
- More than 14 million refugees and displaced persons are living in temporary housing.

Housing Facts

- By the year 2030, 40 percent of the world's population will need access to housing.
- Worldwide, an average of one in three people in cities lives in inadequate housing with only limited access to basic services.
- Since the mid-1990s, only 10 percent of the World Bank's funding has gone to providing housing for people with low incomes.
- Research has shown that building houses creates job opportunities for migrants to cities and encourages the growth of small businesses.

Further Resources

Web Sites

My Sustainable House
http://www.mysusthouse.org/
A Scottish-based interactive game where you can test your environmental awareness and try building a sustainable home for yourself.

Cities Around the World
http://www.globe.veoliaenvironnement.com/globe/en/
Children from 30 countries explore their own cities, discovering their plans for the future and thinking about how to make them more sustainable.

Energy Star Kids
http://www.energystar.gov/index.cfm?c=kids.kids_index
A site full of activities, lesson plans, games, and information for kids on how they can become more energy efficient in their schools and in their homes, helping the planet and saving the environment as they do.

Children of the Earth United
http://childrenoftheearth.org/
Take an adventure in environmental education and learn about Earth issues, view green building videos, take part in fun activities, and much more on this web site.

Newington Sustainable Olympic Village, Sydney
http://www.abc.net.au/science/slab/olympics/default.htm
This article provides a good case study of how a neighborhood can be developed on sustainable principles as a model to others.

The Green Building, South Africa
http://www.sustainable.org.za/greenbuilding/index.htm
Explore a green building in South Africa, built by Sustainable Energy Africa.

BoKlok Housing
www.boklok.co.uk
Find out about this innovative new concept of sustainable housing from the furniture company IKEA.

Books

Belmont, Helen, *Planning for a Sustainable Future* (Geography Skills), Smart Apple Media, 2008

Connolly, Sean, *Safeguarding the Environment* (Campaigns for Change), Smart Apple Media, 2006

McLeish, Ewan, *Sustainable Homes* (Sustainable Futures), Smart Apple Media, 2007

Morgan, Sally, *Natural Resources* (Global Village), Smart Apple Media, 2009

Rae, Alison, *Trees and Timber Products* (Development without Damage), Smart Apple Media, 2010

Rodger, Ellen, *Building a Green Community* (Energy Revolution), Crabtree Publishing, 2008

Royston, Angela, *Buildings of the Future* (Eco-Action), Heinemann Library, 2008

Stringer, John, *Energy* (Sustainable Futures), Smart Apple Media, 2009

Glossary

amenities things that make life comfortable—in communities, these might be buses, shops, or libraries.

aquifer an underground area for storing water.

biogas a mixture of the gases methane and carbon dioxide, which is produced when organic material breaks down or decomposes.

brownfield an area of building development on what was once industrial land.

carpooling a system in which people living in a community arrange to share rides to work, so that the cost of car trips is shared and the environmental impact is less, because there are fewer cars on the roads.

cellulose a wood fiber used in paper making that can be used as a form of insulation in houses.

commute to travel from home to work. Many people commute from suburbs to town or city centers for their jobs.

economy the supply of money gained by a country or community from goods and services.

fossil fuels nonrenewable resources used for fuel that come from the Earth. Fossil fuels include coal, oil, and natural gas.

global warming the name given to the rise in temperatures around the world. Global warming does happen naturally, but some temperature increase is caused by human activity such as burning fossil fuels in cars and industry, which releases greenhouse gases into the atmosphere.

grant a gift of money paid by an organization or government to another organization or individual. Grants do not have to be repaid.

greenhouse gas a gas such as carbon dioxide that can contribute to global warming.

habitat the particular area where certain plants or animals live.

high-density housing groups of houses or apartments that are close together. High-density housing is sustainable because it can house many people, and it also saves on energy.

incentive a plan to encourage people to do something. Often, incentives are grants given by governments that mean people can afford to adopt sustainable solutions.

Industrial Revolution the period in the eighteenth and nineteenth centuries when people began using machines to manufacture goods, causing a dramatic rise in industrial output.

infrastructures the assets a country has that help support its economy, such as water supply, road systems, and power supplies.

insulation anything that helps to keep heat in. In housing, roofs and walls can be insulated using materials including sheep's wool or even paper.

LEDC less economically developed country—one of the poorer countries of the world. LEDCs include all of Africa, Asia (except Japan), Latin America and the Caribbean, Melanesia, Micronesia, and Polynesia.

MEDC more economically developed country—one of the richer countries of the world. MEDCs include the whole of Europe, North America, Australia, New Zealand, and Japan.

megacity a city with more than 10 million people living in it.

photovoltaic cells also called solar cells, special "tiles" that convert light from the sun into electricity to power homes and other buildings.

pollutant anything that pollutes something—air, water, or ground. Pollutants can be gases like carbon dioxide that cause global warming, or chemicals that are released into water supplies during industrial processes.

population density the number of people per square mile of land.

rammed-earth a building technique that uses earth mixed with clay and sand. The mixture is used to fill in a wooden framework and then "rammed" or packed solid, after which the frame is removed, leaving strong walls.

refurbishment the process of changing a house or other building within its existing structure, so it is changed and modernized rather than being demolished.

residential used to describe domestic housing—somewhere people live.

rural relating to the countryside.

sanitation infrastructures that are designed to protect public health. Sanitation includes proper sewage systems and disposal of domestic and industrial waste.

shantytown an unplanned area made up of temporary shelters that often grows up on the outskirts of towns and cities. People who cannot afford housing in city centers often have to live in these areas. There are few facilities in shantytowns.

stormwater runoff the water that is not absorbed by the soil during periods of heavy rainfall.

subsidy money given by a government to encourage people to take a particular action. For example, the Japanese government gave some money toward buying and installing solar panels on houses.

suburb a residential area on the outskirts of a city or town.

sustainability a form of development that benefits a country or community's economy, but also benefits the local environment and the quality of life of its inhabitants.

urban relating to built-up areas such as towns and cities.

urbanization the process in which increasing numbers of people are moving to cities and other urban areas.

urban sprawl the spreading of a city into once-rural areas on its outskirts.

village a settlement or community that is smaller than a town.

wind turbine a device that catches the wind and uses it to power a generator that creates electricity.

Index